From Both Sides of Creation:

Poems of A. J. Mittendorf

In the

beginning,

God created

heaven

and

earth

(Genesis 1:1)

xulon
PRESS

From Both Sides of Creation
Poems of A. J. Mittendorf
by A. J. Mittendorf

Printed in the United States of America

ISBN 9781628710021

BACK COVER: Poem: "On This Image" by A. J. Mittendorf

BACK COVER: Image: The Hubble Space Telescope's "Ultra Deep Field" (courtesy of NASA, 2004) shows an area of space "the size of the head of a pin held at arm's length" and boasts 10,000 galaxies. In fact, everything in the image is a galaxy, except for those one or two points of light with radiating spikes. To photograph the entire night sky with similar images would require 13 million shots like the UDF and centuries' worth of telescope time. The closest galaxies in the image are estimated to be a billion light-years away. The farthest are estimated at some 13 to 15 billion light-years distant.

BACK COVER: layout: Jeremy Barnhart, www.GoldirockEntertainment.com

www.xulonpress.com

Special thanks to my beloved sister, Mary Wolfe (Katy),
who helped me to edit and proofread
all the poems in this volume

and to

Jeremy Barnhart, my friend and fellow labourer
from
www.GoldiRockEntertainment.com
for the cover design for this book.

ABOUT THE AUTHOR

For 25 years, A. J. Mittendorf has taught English to high school and college students in both the United States and Canada. While he has always loved creating with the written word, he didn't begin writing in a formal capacity until age 30, and he now enjoys writing and publishing poetry, essays and short stories. Most recently, two of his short, non-fiction stories were included in a volume assembled by celebrated Canadian author, Stuart McLean: *Time Now for "The Vinyl Café" Story Exchange*, published in 2013 by Viking-Penguin Canada (Toronto).

In addition to writing, A. J. is an accomplished double bassist and music arranger, and an actor, often presenting his own poetry as miniature works of drama. He presently lives on Vancouver Island in British Columbia, Canada.

To my daughter, Bella, and grandson, Dallas:
Two who challenge and inspire me,
and, despite my faults, admire me.

Table of Contents

~~~⌐

Preface

⟋⟍

Using Genesis 1:1 as my guide, I have divided this volume into two sections: The first section—Heaven—is the sacred section, and while it contains fewer poems than the other, it has just as much heart. The second section—Earth—is called the secular section; don't let the name fool you, though; it's not that I delve into debauchery or leap into lechery. The perspective is the same; only the focus changes, but that also doesn't mean that you won't find one or two "naughty" words within. You will. I'm a realist, so I dealt with reality.

So, if the perspective is consistent, why would I make the effort to divide the book? It's simple: I kept my audience–or, rather, *audiences*–in mind, as I was taught to do during all my years as a duteous pupil.

I set the "religious" section first so that those among my readers who have delicate spiritual constitutions can each drop a pebble within the margins of my religiosity and hopscotch past it. Then, those who prefer the spiritual emphasis may religiously anoint the margins of the secular section with blood and "pass over" it. The boldest of you I invite and even dare to read both sections. But for all of you, secular, sacred or some of both, enjoy what you read, be blessed, live long and prosper.

Introduction

I wrote my first poem when I was, maybe, twelve. What made me feel proud of it was not how it sounded as I composed it or as I read the final version. Instead, it was my mother's reaction to reading it aloud. I had left it on the dining room table accidentally, and she read it for a conversation starter during the meal:

> In church you learn,
>> In church you pray,
> In church you sit
>> throughout the day.

I was more than pleased to see her laugh at my quippish little verse, but the laughter of the rest of the family infused loads of encouragement in me, and for the next several weeks I composed pages upon pages of less inspired poems, none of which have survived to the present—thankfully.

As the years progressed I continued to write, but I was far from prolific, mainly, I suppose, because I didn't know what to write about. I took some creative writing courses during my high school years (you can read more about them in the second half of this book), but they did little to help me in that area—gave me nothing that grabbed my attention about writing in general that helped me to write more continuously, despite the encouragement I received from my teachers, so in my high school years and the first years after that, I produced little of consequence.

I was about 22 when I was finally told, in no uncertain terms, that I was to be a writer. I was just learning the benefits of prayer, and in that time I was also reading a collection of poems by Edgar Allan Poe. I was taking my time studying them, wanting to be certain I was able to grasp the meaning of each word in every poem. On one particular day during this time, I prayed, "God, if you want me to be a writer, inspire me to write something." Of course, I was hoping for something that was clearly inspired, not just another A. J. poem.

Later that same day, after I had read Poe's "Eldorado" and had pondered it for a few hours, God responded to my prayer: "Make it Scriptural," he seemed to say. I had already plodded through Poe's poem several times, but when I finally grasped the meaning, I realized that, even though the poem's speaker clearly dies, it is, for Poe, a happy ending, with clear references, however unbiblical, to heaven, and I knew how to remake it in Scripture's image.

Mind you, I ultimately destroyed one of Poe's very few happy endings, and I could never have hoped to top his mastery of language, especially in a first attempt, but, as relatively infantile as it was, my understanding of Heaven and Hell was the impetus, not my relative skill as a poet.

But let me be perfectly frank: I did not want to write that poem. I was telling myself, as I got a few pieces of paper, that it would be stupid. I was complaining, as I grabbed a pen from the desk drawer, that it would be a waste of my time. I groaned aloud as I took a seat at my desk, opened Poe's collection to "Eldorado" and weighted the book flat with a stapler, that it would only keep me up all night. And even as I wrote, I was begrudging the poem's composition, yet I was entirely unable to not write, and it turned out to be something that I was pleased with the next day. I did some revising, and, to be honest, even in its finished version, it's hardly a work of art, but it was the best I'd ever done until then, negative though it may be. Both Poe's and my versions of "Eldorado" are printed at the end of this introduction, so you can have a complete understanding of my experience.

But, it wasn't the puerile quality of my work in comparison with Poe's brilliance that was important. It was the fact that I was compelled to write this poem on the day that I had asked for God to inspire something—and when I distinctly did not want to write it, that, not only got me writing, but has kept me writing for nearly thirty years since. I am a good teacher, but I was called to be a writer. I'm a skilled actor, but I was called to be a writer. I am an accomplished musician, but I was called to be a writer.

Now, you should also understand that my work has been turned down by more magazines than I can count. From the various comments that I have received, (and not every editor has offered comments) I conclude that my work is too literary for religious publications, and too religious for literary publications. That's not a complaint, just a fact. Whether I'm writing short fiction, poetry, essays or drama, that biblical perspective, so pervasive in my being, continues to shine through. So, this is my first collection, and, while it is divided into "Sacred" and "Secular" poems, it all comes from a sacred perspective, in spite of one or two "naughty" words that are used in the second, "Secular," section.

Whenever I wonder why I write, I think of two things: I think, first, of the day when, feeling like some sort of clock-work automaton, I began writing a poem that was based on my own convictions, that expressed my understanding of the biblical concept of heaven—well, and hell, too, in this case. And I think of my mother's reaction to my first poem, how she enjoyed reading it so much that she had to share it, and that it made everyone laugh. You may even notice, Beloved Reader, as you peruse my printed poetic productions, that my sense of humour hasn't changed since that first poem at the opening of this introduction, and I'm glad because I demand three things from my work: First, I demand that it be art—that, regardless of the ideas, they must be artistically presented. Second, I want to express ideas that are original, insightful, pertinent and perhaps even somewhat controversial. Finally, it is my sincere hope, Beloved Reader, that you are blessed by what you read, that you enjoy it. Whether you laugh, scowl, cock your chin to the side and mumble, "Huh," I want you to enjoy reading because, if it's not a joy to read, then what's the point?

Eldorado (Edgar Allan Poe)

Gaily bedight,
A gallant knight,
In sunshine and in shadow,
Had journeyed long,
Singing a song,
In search of Eldorado.

But he grew old–
This knight so bold–
And o'er his heart a shadow
Fell as he found
No spot of ground
That looked like Eldorado.

And as his strength
Failed him at length,
He met a pilgrim shadow–
"Shadow," said he,
"Where can it be–
This land of Eldorado?"

"Over the mountains
Of the moon,
Down the valley of the Shadow,
Ride, boldly ride,"
The shade replied,—
"If you seek for Eldorado!"

Eldorado (A. J. Mittendorf)

A rich Spanish knight,
Quite poor in his sight,
Though his armor did glow,–
This fool he sought,
But all for naught,
The land of Eldorado.

In wealth he was raised;
His money he praised;
He entreated his riches to grow,–
Verily, so verily
I say unto ye,
He'd had his Eldorado.

Upon his life's end
He asked of a friend
Whose name was merely, "Shadow,"
"Where is this land
Of golden sand,
The land of Eldorado?"

But Shadow came
From the eternal flame
And lead the good knight into sorrow.
Eternally
He's in company
Of those kept from Eldorado.

For from one's rebirth
He knows that, on Earth,
There is no Eldorado.
Keep with the Lord,
Be swift with his sword,
For Christ is Eldorado.

Part 1

FROM THE SACRED SIDE
OF CREATION

Poems of
God, the Father; God, the Son;
Heaven and Hell; Creation and Judgement;
Life and Death; Blessings and Curses;
Prayer; Righteousness and Sin

An Appetizer

A poem is an omni-sensory
entrée, and it should be served
as such: on the page like a dish
in the finest, five-star, French restaurant.
It must appeal to the eye
before it can appeal to the palate,
without need of side orders
or dollops of ketchup.
The page is not the poem's medium,
it's the frame—
as the plate is the entrée's frame;
the poem must appear as a portrait,
with a sauce elegantly
painted over,
and a garnish gracefully setting
the sight off centre.

Creation's Blaze Is but a Spark

If god in all his power governed just
Creation's giants—murder, pain, disease,
and all the planets, stars and galaxies—
in such a god I'd surely place my trust.
And if he only moved in bits of dust—
the microscopic specks no human sees—
commanding atoms and such things as these,
revering such a god would be a must.
But both combined could not compare with God
who moves the Christened cosmos with a nod.
The atom and the galaxy?—the same
to God. To God, the mighty and the lame
are one. To God, all human light is dark;
to God, Creation's blaze is but a spark.

From What Is Woman Made?

Is Woman made from Nature's frothy fluff—
the scraps Creation left for time to fade?
What dust was there unused, or from what stuff
    is Woman made?

In Adam's rib such precious gems were laid
that, taken from him, there was just enough
for God to make for him a constant aide;

So all Man's finest attributes—the tough,
the tender, the mighty and the meek—were paid
and placed in her—for him; of this fine stuff
    is Woman made.

The Magnificat
from Luke 1: 46-55

My soul proclaims the greatness of THE LORD!
My spirit celebrates my God and Saviour,
for he has gently looked with mercy toward
my lowly state; I'll praise his name forever!
The Mighty God has done great things for me;
his mercy drops like rain on every age.
The righteous deeds of his right hand decree
that all who fear him will escape his rage,
but those of prideful hearts he has disbanded,
and, like dried leaves, they're strewn about the earth.
He sends away the wealthy empty handed
that they may know what life is really worth.
While God has humbled rulers from their thrones,
he's always good to those whose hearts he owns.

Sex Through Jesus' Eyes

To picture sex through Jesus' eyes,
    contemplate the flower:
It covers Earth with beauty through
    its frailty, not its power.

It bathes her with its comeliness
    and clothes her modestly.
It won't coerce; it won't cajole,
    but offers honestly.

It can't withhold its blessedness
    but gives with all its living.
It bears no malice, holds no grudge,
    but demonstrates forgiving.

It draws one close; none can resist
    the lure of such a treasure—
the sight, the scent, the supple sense
    of this God-given pleasure.

And I would not abuse this gift
    nor with it try to smother;
I'd not reclaim a flower I've given
    to offer to another.

On God's Omnipotence

If God seems overwhelmed by daily strife
and burdened by the constant cares of life,
if he is plagued by wars and talk of wars
and mired by people's doubts when death is rife,
if he's so cumbered by his list of chores
he seems bedeviled by "those prayers of yours"
but finally answers them "to shut you up,"
well, here's a thought this problem underscores:
Your god's a wimp; if I were you, I'd swap;
I serve a god no other god can top.
He gives complete attention, face to face,
to all his children, yet he'll never stop
juggling the woes of folks in every place
with all the infinite minutia of space.

Courier: A Riddle

In its rhyme, this poem, a caddie,
bears the name of God, the Father,
cried by those—and not one other—
close enough to call Him, "Daddy."

Haiku

I slipped through time back
to the Jurassic— "Darkness
there, and nothing more."

Untitled

I set my prayers before THE LORD
    and leave them without guessing.
He will answer "yea" or "nay,"
    and either is my blessing.

I Am More

From Us

In this minuscule immensity of space,
in this mini magnitude of time,
in this tortured blessedness that we call life,
I find myself demanding more.
What more is there that can pack this empty place,
filled with little else than lust for crime,
other than the pointed plunging of a knife?
My heart, my soul insists on more!

To Us

All the vastness of the stars and galaxies,
all the days and eons, eras, ages,
all the helpful deeds, and each unselfish thought,
are only specks. Yes, there's more.
You became a host of living casualties;
that's why your hearts are full of empty pages.
I can ease your pain and fill that vacant grot.
Please, let me have you; I am more.

The Allegory of Soils
(after Matthew 13: 3-9)

A farmer
went to sow.
As he
scattered,
some seed fell
on the path,
and the birds ate it.
Some fell
among rocks,
where there's
not a lot of dirt;
plants shot up
quickly,
but the sun
scorched them,
so they withered
and died.
Some fell
among weeds
that grew up
with the plants
and choked them;
they died, too;
But a little fell on good, dark, moist, healthy, fertile soil
where the seed produced a rich, bountiful crop—
a hundred times what was sown by the farmer's hand;
The farmer and all his family ate well that year and lived.

On Prayer

Imagine for a moment that you kneel
beside the foot of twenty Everests all
about you. These white-haired judges make you feel
a terrifying awe—immensely small.
And yet the sun warms well your trembling flesh,
and water pools about you serving sweet,
delicious drink, while, eager to refresh
you, trees stretch down their fruit for you to eat.
Peaceful fear, frightening bliss to stand
before a mighty God in prayer. But mild,
He spreads titanic love by dreaded hand
and lifts us up as we might lift a child.
As martyrs meet the swinging of the sword,
with fear and joy, we bow before THE LORD.

An Allegory on Sin

My garden lay before me full of weeds,
and, knowing that it could not weed itself,
I knelt to execute my gardener's deeds
and filled a pail with dying green myself.
Before I'd put my tools away, I spied
one final weed but pulled out only half
the root before it broke. In time, it tried
to grow again; again I yanked the chaff.
Six times it peeked; six times I plucked the leaf
a little farther down its root that wound
around a bush's base. Then like a thief,
my seventh try, I stole the whole out of the ground.
But had that weed not made such shows of force,
I never could have snatched it from its source.

The Rape of Lucretia[1]

I never would have noticed them if they
had parked a little further down the lot,
but they stopped right in front of me; I saw
them through the window of the shop where I'd
been watching for my daughter. They were young,
this couple—not a month since graduation,
assuming that they'd graduated yet.
  The boy got out, returning movies next door.
His walk displayed his confidence; he smiled—
the way a wolf might when his belly's full.
  The girl remained alone—as she had been
and as she seemed to feel she'd always feel.
Her braces glistened in the sunlight as
she seemed to grin; her downcast eyes, though, and
her softened spasms gave her heart away.
She never did look up toward the boy,
nor did he ever look to her with love.
(He only took her for a ride, is all.)
  She quickly dried her eyes when he got back;
she feigned a smile and meekly glanced his way,
pretending to be glad of his return,
as though she thought that he'd begin to love
her somewhat if he saw that she was glad.
He spun the wheel, and they both sped away.
  I wish I could have helped her when she cried,
but who am I to her that she'd accept
whatever words of comfort I could give?
What can I do but pray for her, whose name
I never knew, whose face I saw but once?
So I will pray for her, and who knows?
I might accomplish more for her with prayer
than with whatever wisdom I might share.

So Distant from Me

I look down on my love, so distant from me;
she bears affections inconsistent with me.

She goes about her day, this way and that,
concerned with matters nonexistent in me.

She lives and lets me live outside herself;
I wonder why she's so resistant to me.

I send her word again, again, again . . .
through faithful messengers—assistants for me.

She leaves me home and runs to former loves
but finds my silence inconsistent of me.

And yet, by heaven, my love—despite the pain
and suffering she brings—demands persistence from me.

I'll send my Spirit deep within her, then,
all Joyful, we'll be self-consistent in me.

Noah's Limerick

They scoffed when they saw Noah's boat:
"There's no water on which it can float!"
    "You're all gunna die,
      not my family and I,"
Noah said (but that's not quite a quote).

Easter

Easter
isn't just some
other celebration
like its pampered baby brother
Christmas;
that, too, brings light,
but glory bathes all Earth
from the Resurrection Might of
Easter.

On Freedom

I had strings, but now I'm free; there are no strings on me.
—From Walt Disney's *Pinocchio*.

Pinocchio dreamed of freedom all his life.
Then late one night, a fairy with a knife
crept lightly up to him: "Because Geppetto
is always kind, I grant you what your strife
will never quite be able to bestow."
She cut his strings, each at the eyelet, "Go,
my little friend; you're free to chase your dream,"
and then she vanished.
                    He woke years ago—
completely liberated—with the beam
of dawn blistering his ever-staring gleam,
and he lay limp and lifeless in its rays;
he could not turn away nor could he scream.
So, in his freedom now that puppet lays
forgotten, and so he shall for all his days.

The Seventh Day

. . . In the end, God,
having glorified His name
in all the earth, said,
"Let us bring together
the seed of Adam and Eve
to divide the children from the
Children." And it was so.
God brought together
every offspring of Eve and Adam
to sift the unbelieving from the
Believing;
and God called the believing, "sheep,"
and the unbelieving he called, "goats."
And God removed the goats from
His Presence and restored the sheep unto
a New Earth and the Joy of THE LORD.
And God saw to it
that everything was very good;
and that was evening,
then there was morning—
The Eighth Day.

A Brief Romance in Hell

*. . . a mighty windstorm struck the mountain so hard
that rocks were broken loose, but THE LORD was not in the wind.*
—from 1 Kings 19:11 NIV

Alone, both all alone for centuries
while baptized in a sea of agonies,
they gasped to glimpse another of their kind
and triumphed in a fleeting drop of ease.
As currents drove their joining, they entwined
but thrust themselves apart. The damned soon find
that love in Hell is hotter yet than all
that burning lake; all comfort is declined.
Then in their clenched hearts, they, who'd had the gall
to see a miracle on Earth and call
it "chance," demanded, "God, why raise the bar
of torture here?" But God heard no such bawl.
How sad that we see Chance when God's not far,
and see God blamed when He's not where we are.

THE LORD Converses with the Devil

You, Satan! Come! Sit here while I speak!
I'm done with all your wicked ways for good.
So from now on you keep your tricks and bleak
conceits out of my children's hearts, and should
I find among my kin a single friend
of yours, by Grace! I'll boot him out as well.
No buts! Of you and yours I've made an end,
so leave my sight; go pester those in Hell—
Don't interrupt. I haven't finished yet—
Take with you Pride, Adultery, Anger, Greed,
and Envy, Sloth, and Gluttony. Forget
how great you were; it's finished, I've decreed;
for I have made both Earth and Heaven new;
in this new age, I give no place for you.

Philippians 2: 5-11
a paraphrase

Your attitude should be the same as Christ's,
who, though he was in very nature God,
refused to make an idol of his godliness,
but poured himself into a servant's mold
and carried up the nature of a man.
And as a man, he humbled himself more,
submitting even to the curse of death—
a death as slow and painful as the cross!
So God exalted him beyond the heights,
presenting him a name above all names,
that at the name of Jesus every knee
should bow—in Heaven, Earth and under Earth—
and every tongue confess that Jesus Christ
is Lord, to glorify our father, God.

When I Have Lain This Body Down . . .

. . . throw me an extravagant funeral:
Dress my bloodless cadaver
in a black tuxedo
with a pleated silk shirt, gold cuff links,
and a velvet bow tie.
Lay my body on padded satin
in a hand-crafted coffin adorned with
opposing Cherubim and Christ's Passion
along a sculpted frieze[2] beside
sparkling brass handles
on a grand mahogany casing.
Hire professional mourners
and have a reception catered with
the finest multi-cultural cuisine.
Make me Pharaoh;[3] deify me
and know that if I'm allowed,
I shall look down on you from Heaven
and scoff.

Should you wish to honour me,
do only what is necessary—
if cremation is cheaper,
cremate, if burial,
buy cheap:
find the least expensive coffin—
used, maybe—
and pack my body in there naked.
(Sell the suit.)
If you want a reception,
have smokies, crackers with
Kraft individually-wrapped cheese
and grocery-store wine.
Do nothing extra
because I'll not attend the funeral;
I won't be in the coffin,
and I will never
be placed
in the
ground.

On Mama's Quilt
Inspired by a true story

We sat together on Mama's quilt,
    my little girl and I;
she raised her tear-filled eyes and asked me,
    "Why did Mama die?

"Isn't Jesus powerful?
    Did he hear our prayers?
Why won't Jesus give her back?
    I wonder if he cares."

"Of course he cares!" I told my girl.
    "He cares for everyone!
But God has plans for each of us—
    You'll see when it's all done."

I pointed out a picture then
    on the quilt her mama made.
It showed the sun emerging from
    behind a storm cloud's shade:

"Our prayers are like this piece of quilt—
    part of a greater whole.
Since we can't see or know it all,
    we trust him, heart and soul."

She could understand that thought,
    accepting it at last.
We cried for Mama, she and I,
    and moved on from the past.

House of Mourning

Once on a dismal-gray autumn day,
while riding alone on horseback,
I passed a gloomy granite chapel
with accusing Gothic windows
set in thick, unforgiving walls
founded on a field of dead weeds and weeping willows.
Beside it lay an unfenced cemetery
adorned with slabs of concrete, marble,
eroded memories,
and the hush of morning rain.
A group stood there with lowered eyes—
some shrouded with dark umbrellas pressing against
    sloping shoulders,
others with water-soaked sleeves
and the Daily News draped across their heads.
As a black and white man came to usher them in,
I wondered,
Do they know they have a spot reserved?

Pontius Pilate

While Pilate sits with drink, Herod enters.

Ah, Herod, my old friend, you're here; good.
I've much enjoyed your hospitality
while you were gone. Please, sit. Let us discuss
the challenges of ruling this rugged land.
The sun burns hot lately, don't you agree?
As if enraged against this nation's pilot;
it scorches me when I direct; I tire
of the struggle. But you and I, we two
have always worked together well, and all
the people see our bond and fear us both
for we are one, as when we rid ourselves
of Jesus Christ, that man of Nazareth.
        Tell me . . . are you at all disturbed by that?
        I tell you, Herod, this land is mine. God gave
this land to me[4] to rule with no one. So
who is this Jesus that they all see him
as king? I see you share this sentiment.
Feeling threatened by a peasant, are
we? Well, fear not my friend; He's gone. We
had little difficulty purging him
from every inch of Caesar's mighty empire;
his loving subjects did the deed for us,
after all, I was willing to
return him. They insisted—"Crucify,"
and "Crucify!" with all the unity
of the gods. So let the guilt fall on their heads.
        If not on theirs, then surely on his own.
I swear that he was silent like a stone
with me; he made not one request of me—
no cries for mercy or to spare his life—
I could have done much more than that, you know.

46

So, let his blood be on his own two hands;
I won't accept responsibility;
his friends refused it; so will I.
                                    His friends.
The earth indeed is lucky not to have
such faithful satellites as these, or she'd
have none at all. Not even gravity
of death could pull them in as his support.
He died wholly alone. When danger seeks
new territory, these fools think with just
their legs. Only the bravest man among
them came to me—after he died—to claim
his body. Bold as sheep, that's what they are.
If they cannot be bothered, neither will I.
Since they left him to die, I'll let his death
fall to their conscience; I'll have none of it.
        Am I a Jew, Herod? What says your law
about the Christ? Is he not a lamb,
a sacrifice for your altar? I hear
these things in passing only; are they true?
I'm asking as a time-honored friend,
withhold nothing; I will be told. Yes?
Yes. Then he was to be killed anyway,
and I did nothing that was not already
to be done. You see? Your law is guilty
and makes me innocent. Blame your law,
or blame your god who wrote the law that sentenced
him to die for weary and disturbed
people . . .
            . . . For the Jews. He died for you,
Herod; you're to blame; not I. Thank
you for your time, my friend; I've learned all that
I need. And now, if you'll excuse me, I
have much to contemplate to rule this land.

The light remains on Pilate. Herod exits.

47

Limerick Sequence

I

The half-lighted orbs found in space
are pictures of us in God's grace:
　　Though darkness surrounds us
　　the light will astound us—
Just turn and behold the sun's face.

II

Unless a seed on the ground dies,
it lives all alone where it lies.
　　But if it deceases
　　the plant it releases
bears fruit of a far greater size.

III

Christ's grave spot was less of a tomb
than a fertile, impregnated womb.
　　Like a seed in the Earth
　　his death became birth—
perpetual, glorified bloom.

IV

The Church by the Saviour is sought;
by only his blood is it bought;
　　If salvation were won
　　by the works we had done,
then Christ and his death are for naught.

V

Obeying the law as a goal
won't help you in saving your soul.
    If you slip in one part,
    despite a good start,
you're guilty of breaking the whole.

VI

If Jesus can die and be raised,
he's one to be worshiped and praised.
    And since it is thus,
    then the glory for us
is to stand in his presence amazed.

VII

Satan glares down at the Church—
A vulture agaze from its perch.
    But Christ gives protection
    by his resurrection;
he won't leave us out in a lurch.

VIII

Christ will return for his bride;
forever she'll stand at his side.
    All dressed in pure white,
    she's clean in his sight;
it's for this one cause that he died.

La Pietá

I wish I'd been there at Gethsemane
with Jesus.
I want to share his tears
and sweat blood with him.
I want to kneel with him,
cry with him,
fear with him,
pray with him—
     be indignant with him.

I don't want to find
profound things to say
to encourage him;
as impossible as it seems,
I just want to let my silent presence
strengthen him.

But I live now, not then,
and I'm only a man
like each of the eleven—
I would probably
just fall asleep too.

I Dreamed a Dream

In my thirst
I came upon the thing:
an ancient, gnarled, monstrous tree;
From it, dangling between Earth and Heaven,
A mighty Rock, too large to lift, bound and beaten.
Beside the tree, a gruesome man
in black suit with top hat and bow tie;
In hand, a sapling—long, pliable, serpentine.

An amicable greeting: a bow, a smile and
sudden fury as three times he whipped the Rock
with the sapling;
I smirked to see so slight a sapling
used against so great a Rock.

He folded his hands, his smile returning,
as wine poured from the three tiny wounds in the Rock.
I gorged myself on a single sip of this New wine

then backed away,
a terrible thing came about:
the Rock crumbled into sand
and fell to the Earth.
A multitude with me suddenly
wept, for the Rock was no more—

but a child stepped forward;
we watched him Take and Eat
a piece of rock and smile with great joy.
We each ate a single grain and were filled
with such joy that we embraced;
in our embrace, the Rock is,
once again, made whole.

This Is My Final Visit to Your Grave

This is my final visit to your grave
because I don't believe that you've been here
to hear my lamentations or give ear
to the countless, tear-filled good-byes that I gave.
So why should I, who knows you're absent, rave,
in visits to the soulless ground each year,
on how you're missed, your memory held so dear?
It's all been said; all future cries I waive.
For if there is a River Styx, you've crossed;
if ever angels come to take away
believing souls, they've taken yours, I say.
But if I'm wrong, nothing's changed; you're lost.
So whether you're in Heaven or in Hell,
until my body lies with yours, farewell.

Part 2

FROM THE SECULAR SIDE OF CREATION

Poems of
Art and Science, History and Mythology,
Pain and Joy, Human Nature,
Life and Death, Heroes and Villains,
Families and Individuals,
Mystery, Wonderment and Confusion

One of my poems has a long history for its creation. While this book is a collection of poetry, I thought that it would be important, where this particular poem is concerned, for you, Beloved Reader, to understand how it developed. So I have included the poem, in all its revisions, in this essay so that you may enjoy, not just the poem, but the process of creation. I wrote the article about ten years ago, so the conclusion is out of date, but the sentiments are the same. If you wish, you may skip this article and go directly to the poem that follows. Otherwise, Beloved Reader, please enjoy.

How "Round About" Came About

"Round About" is just a tiny, nine-line poem, but it took almost thirty years to complete it. The finished product is siamese-twin cinquains[1]. That is to say, after joining two cinquains so that the last line of the first became the first line of the next, "Round About" was born. I was able to keep all the drafts, so every once in a while I read them over to reminisce, to watch the poem grow, as it were, as if the drafts were photos of me at various stages of my development, not unlike watching the growth of a flower in time-lapse photography. By itself, this little poem is so small, I could easily have lost it at any stage if it weren't for the fact that people (specifically, my dad and all of my teachers who read it) continued praising it, prompting me to care for it and intermittently revise it, like someone periodically returning to sculpt a Bonsai[2].

It began as an assignment in my grade-eight creative writing course in 1977 under the tutelage of Alma Reinecke. She assigned the class to write a

---

[1] Cinquain: in this case, an unrhymed, syllable-count poem invented by Adelaid Crapsey (1878–1914) in which each of its first four lines has two syllables more than the previous line; it begins and ends with two-syllable line.

[2] Bonsai: an Asian potted tree that is kept small by its placement it in a shallow dish and by the continued pruning and shaping of its branches.

Diamanté[3] or something similar. I recall very little about the assignment, but I do remember being displeased with the result. I hadn't the maturity to identify the problem with it, but looking back, I see that my intuition was telling me that it was underdeveloped— awkward. All it needed was a little time and some shaping, but I couldn't have known that then, having yet written nothing of consequence; I knew only that I was dissatisfied with it. It read like this:

Rock
round, grey
sits, thinks, watches
falls and breaks
Sand.

Initially, I would have been eager to forget all about it, but Mrs. Reinecke commented before the class that it was "the most beautiful thing [I'd] written" until then that semester. I remember those words like I do my first kiss. That little, nameless rock poem was ultimately printed in the class's writing journal, "The Inspiration Point," an assemblage of what we had collectively determined to be our best work during the course. It was only a hastily-planned, mimeograph handout that went to each pupil in the class, but it's something of a small treasure for me; I still have my copy.

In 1981, during my senior year of high school, I enrolled in another creative writing course taught by Vera Sadler. She introduced the class to the cinquain using several examples by Adelaide Crapsey, and, as an in-class assignment that day, she had us each compose one of our own. I cheated. I simply revived my rock poem from Mrs. Reinecke's class. She had liked it, after all, and it was similar in form to what Mrs. Sadler wanted, so it would only take a little work to make it conform to her requirements. I recreated it from memory then reworked it. It remained untitled, but by the end of the class, the poem felt distinctly less awkward than it had. The first revision of my rock poem is this:

---

[3] Diamanté: an unrhymed formulaic poem consisting of an odd number of lines (usually seven), emphasizing number of words, rather than number of syllables per line. It begins with a noun in the first line, then two adjectives, three participles, then four nouns; the first two refer to the opening idea; the other two refer to the closing idea. Then the process reverses until you close with a noun which contrasts with the opening noun. The form was invented in 1969 by Dr. Iris M. Tiedt (b. 1928).

A Rock
Will sit and think,
Will fall then crack and break,
And spread along the ocean's beach
As Sand.

My effort paid off. Mrs. Sadler praised my rock poem as a lovely creation, and at home, at the advice of my father, I stored it in my footlocker, tucked inside my copy of "The Inspiration Point." There, in one of my rare attempts at adolescent organization, both versions of my rock poem lay until they were once again called upon.

After graduation, I attempted two years of college, did miserably, joined the navy for four years and revived my college career late in 1987. In yet another creative writing class, this one under the direction of Dr. Mary Prior, my class was assigned to compose, by a defined and distant deadline, 100 lines of poetry (of various forms and types, preferably). I started writing late on the eve of the due date. Having decided against the very tempting idea of reviving a load of gibberish from my navy days, realizing that, with Dr. Prior's high standards, those less-than-clean, less-than-intelligent pieces would produce a decidedly lower mark than any actual writing I might do, I sat myself at the dining-room table and, in several very long hours, composed a dreadfully poor ballad that turned out to be a cloying love story: boy sees girl from afar; boy loves girl from afar; boy continues to love girl from afar; the end.

Upon completion of this piece, after packing as many words into that already weak plot as possible, stretching it to the point of snapping, I had 23 four-line stanzas—92 poorly written lines. My brain had grown numb, but, having consumed an entire pot of coffee, I was also unable to sleep. So I changed my mind, looked through the stuff in my footlocker and retrieved both versions of my rock poem. If used, it would bring my line count to 97. Definitely an 'A,' if the poetry had been any good, but since it wasn't, I still needed at least three additional lines in order to pass the unit, and I knew that I was able to pass.

After rereading both versions, I started contemplating the word "as" in the last line of the second version: "As Sand," and it occurred to me that, in context, it meant, "in the form of:" the rock spreads along the beach "*in the form of* sand." But it could mean "while," if something were happening simultaneously; it could also mean "like," if there were a comparison. What was really exciting, though, was the realization that "as" could mean all three at the same time. I began playing with contrasts: if the rock is alone, then grains of sand must unite; if the rock breaks apart, the sand must coalesce, and so on. Grabbing pen and paper, I slowly created four additional lines—a second cinquain that started with the last line of the first, and which took almost as long to write as the entire ballad had. The continuation of the form emphasized the similarity of the processes discussed in the poem, while the contrast of the processes added interest to the poem itself; if nothing else, joining the two cinquains, I figured, would show some amount of thought, while my ballad, I knew, would not. My rock poem grew into this:

> A rock
> Will sit and think;
> Will fall then crack or break,
> And spread along the ocean's beach
> As sand
> Will congregate;
> Will meet and greet in hoards,
> And settle in their shrinking rooms
> As stone.

101 lines of poetry! I don't remember what I called the ballad, but to my rock poem I proudly assigned the title "Round About." I earned a 'C-' in that poetry unit and an 'A-' for the course itself, thanks, once again, to my rock poem. In her comments, Dr. Prior praised it because "it acts out the title." After some appropriately pointed chastisement about my pathetic ballad, she also suggested that "Round About" was ready for publication as is. That was three for three.

By the end of 1990, I decided that it was time I entered something in my University's literary magazine, *Red Weather*. Proudly remembering Dr. Prior's comments on "Round About," I once again dug it out, and, seeing that it could still use a spruce up, I made more carefully considered revisions. I decided that the poem should begin and end as similarly as possible for the sake of unity, but I rejected the idea of ending the poem with the clumsy phrase "As rock," so I changed the opening instead with pleasing results. Further, to accentuate the contrast between the solitude of the rock and the coming together of the sand, I altered the second line, despite the inadvertent rhyme that resulted.

Finally, in an attempt to more accurately represent the on-going processes of rock becoming sand and sand becoming rock, I removed the period at the close, so that the poem is without end; when you get to the bottom, you can go back to the top. "Round About" blossomed:

Round About

A stone
Will stand alone,
Will fall then crack or break
And spread along the ocean's beach
As sand
Will congregate,
Will meet and greet in hoards
And settle in their shrinking rooms
As stone

When it was printed in *Red Weather*, in the spring of 1991, the person who did the typesetting discovered that she had some extra space after the poem, so she rearranged the lines without consulting me. What had been a nine-line poem became a thirteen-line poem. It filled the page but devastated the writer. Even so, "Round About" was praised by faculty and fellow students alike. Even Dr. Prior congratulated me in the halls of the English department. All that affirmation coupled with the reworked typesetting prompted me to further develop the poem in order to publish it again some time in the future. I wasn't finished yet.

"Round About" lay dormant for some thirteen years, until I finally got my writing career under way. When I read it then, I found myself again not entirely satisfied. Sand can spread out on more beaches than just those by the ocean; the idea needed to be more universal, so I changed "ocean's beach" to "water's edge" in line four. In line eight, I changed "their," referring to the sand, to "its," simply because it's grammatical, and I changed "rooms" to "room" to accentuate singleness in preparation for the close. In this version, "Round About" appears as the following:

Round About

A stone
Will stand alone,
Will fall then crack or break,
And spread along the water's edge
As sand
Will congregate,
Will meet and greet in hoards,
And settle in its shrinking room
As stone

There is an old-fashioned rule for poetry, demanding capital letters at the opening of each line; my adherence to that rule ultimately waned as I continued to mature. Even as my hair line receded, so the upper-case letters in all of my poetry was combed out, including those in "Round About." Its appearance in *Red Weather* was its last in anything largely public. I printed it in a chapbook—a Christmas present for friends and family in 2004; otherwise it's been just for me, until now. But even for my chapbook I found room to strengthen my little poem; it now appears in its mature form as follows:

Round About

a stone
will stand alone,
will fall then crack or break
and spread along the water's edge
as sand
will congregate,
will meet and greet in hoards
and settle in its shrinking room
as stone

Reliving the various versions of "Round About" has become for me like watching the movement of a character in a flip-book cartoon, each version reflecting my level of growth as an aspiring writer, each one a snap-shot of my life at the time it was written.

In years to come, when I begin losing hair or teeth or memory or marbles, "Round About" may begin to lose lines or syllables; maybe it's as developed as it will get; who knows? George Lucas teaches us that a work of art is never completed, it's ultimately abandoned. So I'm not going to worry what will happen to it, but I do often wonder what would have happened to "Round About" if Mrs. Reinecke hadn't taken notice of my rock poem, or if she had just held her tongue back in 1977. Would I have thrown it away? Surely, I would never have submitted it to the class for inclusion in "The Inspiration Point," to say nothing of reviving it for Mrs. Sadler four years later. And if she hadn't also praised it, would I have bothered saving it in my footlocker? I might very well have dismissed it and left it lying around the house for my mother to throw away. It surely would have been long forgotten before I enrolled in Dr. Prior's class, if, in fact, I enrolled at all. And if she hadn't been honest in her assessment of my ballad, her praise of "Round About" may have meant much less. Surely, if she hadn't cared to comment on "Round About" at all, I would never have had enough confidence to submit it to *Red Weather*. In the thirty-year creation of "Round About," it was always the honest, open praises from those whom I respect that kept it going. It was their encouragement that gave me the desire to revive and revise, develop and grow. It was their praises that made that poem what it is today: new, distinct, ripe, and alive.

An Addendum

It is summer of 2013 when the book you are now holding, Beloved Reader, is just about to go to press. I have been re-reading the text in the search of errors, booboos and blunders. One can never eliminate them all—not on this side of eternity, anyway, but while I was re-reading the above article, I actually found myself thinking, "'Round About' is done; there will be no more changes," despite my thoughts at the close of the article above. As I read the last version though, just before the conclusion, I realized that I wasn't happy with the idea that the first and last lines aren't identical. "Well, they're only one letter off," I argued with myself. "It's imperfect like life is imperfect, so why be bothered?" But then I realized that, I can begin with "as stone," like the last line, if I change the "as" in line five to "so," and add a comma to the end of line four. Rather than beginning with an assertion and ending with the analogy, I know now that I can begin with an analogy and conclude with the assertion. Such little changes can bring about so much difference!

After 36 years, my poem is still developing, and even I am surprised by its continued growth. The poem–in its most recent revision–is on the following page. You never know, it may change again as time moves onward. I doubt it, but then, I've doubted it before.

Round About

as stone
will stand alone,
will fall and crack or break
and spread along the water's edge,
so sand
will congregate,
will meet and greet in hoards
and settle in its shrinking room
as stone

On Literature

If you're not smiling when you read my stuff,
then I'm not doing my job well enough,
for, since it's meant to share the poet's wit,
a poem amounts to little more than fluff.
Once someone argued through clenched teeth to spit:
"Hey, watch your mouth! Poetry's serious shit!
How dare you stoop to slander your own art?!"
I answered, "I love every form of lit,—
but listen, can it lift the heavy heart
of one who's lost to grief? Can it start
construction on a home? Can it feed
the hungry? Clothe the naked? Or impart
a life? Since lit can meet no real need,
it should, at least, be worthy of the read."

Gleeful Mêlée

I was at my friend's house
just the other day—
(it seems so, anyhow).
We had known each other
for only the day,
but we were best friends
and we knew it
and you couldn't have
changed our minds for nothin'—
that's for darn sure!
His brother was there that evening,
and he was older than my friend
I bet by forty years—
(He was married and had a baby)!
But he loved a good fight
'cause he and my friend
wrestled and kicked and laughed,
red-faced with glee,
in the middle of the living room—
right there in the middle of it!—
with the mom and dad right there too!
The mom said, "Oh! You two boys . . ." but they
wrestled and laughed, wrestled and laughed.
I admit that I was a little confused,
but when I could finally stand it no longer,
I couldn't help myself—
I jumped right in among the gleeful mêlée.

Runaway

Around the cape and quietly
    our wounded ship took flight
and sailed to sea like one gone mad,
    beyond the speed of sight.

The sails took hold of whispered wind
    as we might gather rain
from tiny pools in desert dirt
    and drink as those insane.

That ship, she led her course alone
    ahead, resolved and doomed!
with none to steer and none to drive—
    with all her crew marooned!

The New Myth

A prophesy on Thetis warned King Zeus,
"Her future off-spring will be greater than
his father. Lord, forbid her to seduce
you; let her couple only with a man."[5]
But Zeus ignored this timely divination.
He lay with Thetis and begot a god
who grew in deed, in lore, and in his station
more mighty than his father, as was told.
(Now, Zeus usurped his throne from Kronos, who
usurped his father's, too.[6] But Zeus's son
surpassed them all in wisdom when he knew
that he would leave this legacy to none.)
Adorned for war before the throne and crown,
he drew his sword and knelt to lay it down.

Papa's Waltz

Croquet is his game—
or so he thinks—but even
when he begs the ball,
gesturing with hips and hands,
it seldom finds the wicket.

The Year's First Snowfall

The year's first snowfall:
rosy noses; gleaming cheeks;
rapid, misty breath—
best of all, through frosty panes,
my children's playful laughter.

The Broken Handle

The broken handle
of an ancient axe
lay decaying
in the dewy shade of
a satisfied, old oak:
"*Sic semper
proditores*,"[7]
the tree remarked.

As I was researching WWI aces for the poem "The Death of the Ace" (placed later in this book), I stumbled upon the picture and biography of this fellow, Eugene Bullard, who was listed among U. S. war pilots. His picture is what caught my attention, clearly, because he was Black, and that fact led me to read his biography with intense assiduity because the question in my mind nagged: How could an African American have gained such a respected position in that particular era? Remember, this was still a generation before the red-tailed planes of WWII, and those who manned them still didn't get the respect they deserved as men, as soldiers or as pilots. If they had, there would have been no red tails at all. I was immediately struck with admiration for this man who had somehow achieved what so many never would, and many others who would achieve this level of respect, needed to wait some sixty years.

Now, I'm also a teacher of literature, and when I read about Bullard, I immediately thought about Phillis Wheatley, whose poetry I had studied, admired and taught, and I knew I had to pair these two remarkable people somehow. So, after a few years of pondering, I finally penned the following two sonnets: the first in honour of Bullard, the second in honour of Wheatley.

I want you to understand, Beloved Reader, that I initially, I wanted to name the first one "The Ace of Spades" because of the obvious puns on both "ace" and "spade;" it was not my intention to malign this man. On the contrary, I was hoping that the racist imagery would highlight what Bullard had overcome in order to fly. I asked a few of my friends, and no one I knew, regardless of their heritage, was comfortable with the ethnic slur, despite my good intentions, and that's understandable. After all, I wouldn't have felt compelled to ask for other people's opinions if their less-than-positive reactions weren't a possibility I had considered. They understood my reasoning and could see the logic, but I decided, based on their valuable input, that it was simply inappropriate, so I dropped the title and began searching for another. It was finally my brother, the consummate aviation afficionado, who suggested the title, "Ace of SPAD's," which still has the ring of "Spade" without the direct slur, but also hints at the fact that Bullard flew with loyalties toward a country other than his own.

Please also understand, Beloved Reader, that I am not afraid of writing something that might be offensive to some if I feel that the message is that important. In this case, I wanted to honour this man, and the potential offense might have hindered that important message. For that reason alone, I changed the title.

The Ace of SPADs

Now here's a man whom we should all revere,
one who deserves some military cheer:
He flew and fought, despite his knightly race,
and ultimately earned the title, "Ace."
His triumph, though, came not just from the war
but through the scorn all non-Caucasians bore:
While grounded by the U. S. airborne lads,
he flew for France. Behold the Ace of SPADs.[8]
Let's lift our cups to Eugene Bullard,[9] he
whose mother's ancestry was from the Cree,
whose father was of African descent.
Salute this man's American Ascent.
No matter where you go or what you do,
allow this person to enliven you.

The 'Noble' Prize Winner

Now here's a lass who—no one can dispute—
has earned the right of everyone's salute,
for she was both a woman and a slave
and in such time when either one was grave.
Named 'Phillis'[10] for the ship that brought her here,
the Wheatley's bought this child who shed no tear.
She turned her back against her homeland dust
and turned her training into Christian trust
that turned her thoughts to touch hearts of such men
as George the Third and General Washington.
And none had guessed that such nobility
would find a home in one so low as she.
No matter where you go or what you do,
allow this person to enliven you.

He Kept on Getting High

He thought that he would live forever;
    he thought he'd never die.
But since he saw his friends pass on,
    he kept on getting high.

He bought his drugs from hooded men
    who walk the streets at night.
They smiled to see him dropping by.
    (My God, but they're polite!)

And, oh! they'd give him such a deal
    if he'd buy on the spot;
if not, well, they knew other guys
    who'd take what he could not.

"Alright, I'll buy it all," he said.
    "Here's every cent I have,
and I'll go floatin' off somewhere
    like someone's run-off slave."

They counted up their hard-earned cash
        and split it all between'em,
"Oh, he'll be back," they told themselves,
        but he'd no longer need'em.

He hid himself in "Warehouse World,"
        abandoned since the war,
and in a hole on the top-most floor
        he drugged like never before.

He'd never been so high; he thought
        he'd challenge natural laws
and float through the air with the greatest of ease
        but killed himself because

he thought that he would live forever;
        he thought he'd never die.
In spite of seeing his friends pass on,
        he kept on getting high.

For Sale: One Time Machine, Never Used

Within a decade's worth of spare time
I built a time machine from compu-scraps
around the house. It should be working fine,
but when I try to travel back, it snaps:
"A paradox!" A time machine, it seems,
can know no time before its own invention.
And forward jaunts? "Anomaly!" it screams;
the future isn't party to creation.
I thought to wait some fifty years or so
and travel back to now, but scoffed, "I'm here
already! What would coming back here show?
I'll just take lots of pictures, and, to clear
away this foolishness, I'll sell my wasted
time machine for what I have invested."

The Ballad of John Maynard
(after Horatio Alger)

John Maynard, he grew with a broad ocean view
    where a boy's bedroom window should be.
His mother washed dishes; his father caught fishes,
    but John, how he cherished the sea!
Now, John was no failure, but served on a whaler—
    his father's command at the time.
At fourteen years old, this boy was as bold
    as a salt who would kill for a dime.

Each night after chow, he sat down at the prow
    to give up some time with his dad.
And the times were not rare when his father would share,
    "I'm proud and impressed with you, Lad.
I knew at your birth that you'd be of great worth;
    you've exceeded my uttermost dream.
You work well alone, but I've also known
    you to work well as part of a team.

"Each task that you do is as fine as the crew,
    and you're at it as long as there's sun.
When you finish a job, you're not one to hob-nob
    if there's even one task left undone.
You're tougher than oak and (this is no joke),
    the men are all betting on you:
They'll take one on the chin if you're not 'tucked in'
    before their working day is all through."

"If I've made you proud, it's because I'm allowed
    to sail the ocean's white foam.
When I sleep on the shore, I'm aware of it more:
    the ocean is really my home.
I want to live here much more year after year;
    the sea has been calling for me!
I want to grow old with a bunk in the hold
    and then die and be buried at sea."

Before a year passed, John's father amassed
    foul lesions where once he had flesh.
With John at his side, he choked and he died;
    John wrapped his remains up in mesh.
He shed not a tear, but he gathered the gear;
    the crew brought the body on deck.
They weighted the cover and dropped the corpse over
    while John kept his crying in check.

Urged on by the crew (all the people he knew)
    he took some time off to revive.
He needed some time to return to his prime—
    to push for and follow his drive.
And having no other, he mourned with his mother;
    they prayed until peace had returned.
Then in spite of her plea, he returned to the sea
    and promised to send all he earned.

With all he possessed in his father's sea chest
    he boarded the ship, *Ocean Queen.*
While seemingly scrawny, he'd prove himself brawny—
    at sea he's the farthest from green.
A year at the most he stood well his post;
    and, humbled, he slaved for each meal.
He made no complaint, but toiled as a saint
    before Cap' tried him out at the wheel.

On Lake Erie's tide his skills were first tried
    in the summer of nineteen-thirteen.
While most of the crew, and the passengers, too,
    reclined on the deck of the *Queen*
(in sunshine so warm raining down on the swarm,
    and the steamer careening her way),
below decks, unseen by those folks so serene,
    black Death went on stalking his prey.

A sailor, wide-eyed, called the captain aside
    to give him the unpleasant word:
"A flame from the furnace will burn to the surface."
    Cap' turned ghostly white when he heard.
He saw it first-hand. No human command
    could rescue the ship's oaken frame.
It showed in his voice that he had no choice
    but surrender the ship to the flame.

With a pulsating heart, Cap' studied the chart,
    assessing the distance from land.
And wiping his brow he whispered a vow:
    "I'll save these folks' lives if I can.
The southern-most beach lies just within reach;
    it's ten minutes out at the most,
With all boilers burning and all engines turning,
    I'll run her aground on the coast.

"Helm, head her south-east!" cried the Captain in haste.
    "Head her south-east right now, at full speed!
Let praying abound that we run her aground!
    There's no hope if we don't succeed!"
And John said, "Aye aye!"—a stately reply—
    as he steered the *Queen* on to his fate.
With unwavering hand he turned straight to the land
    for patrons and crew—the *Queen*'s freight.

And under his breath, as he headed for death,
    he said, "Dad, are you proud of me still?"
A touch on his shoulder made John Maynard bolder;
    he found his task almost a thrill.
He remembered with pride the first time that he tried
    to pilot a ship with his dad.
He said, "Son, it's innate. The ship's your soul mate!
    With all that you do I am glad."

With flames ever nearing, John kept right on peering
    through air comprised mostly of smoke.
"John, how are you fairing?" Cried Cap', always caring.
    "Here, cover your nose with my cloak.
A mile or two more till we're safely ashore!
    Can you make it that long, my good man?"
"If the ship can hold out, then there is no doubt.
    Just watch me; I'm sure that I can."

"Just five minutes yet to the end of the threat;
    Keep going, John, five minutes still!"
With the flames burning through to the sole of his shoe,
    "Aye Captain, with God's help I will!"
"Just one moment on you'll be finished, dear John!
    Just one moment more at the wheel!"
With a plunge and a thrust, they were tossed to the dust
    when the stones grated under the keel.

"Give thanks unto God!" cried the uninjured squad,
    those saved from the sea and the flame.
John never did reel, but stood strong at the wheel
    until striking the mark of his aim.
What a most fitting pyre was the dying ship's fire;
    a hero he ever will be
who gave up his ghost for the *Ocean Queen*'s host—
    when John Maynard perished at sea.

Double Dactyl

Do-Re-Me, A-B-C
Alfred John Mittendorf
studies the basics; he'll
master them yet!

Working with numbers, now,
that's where his challenge is.
Math-e-ma-tic-al-ly,
Alfred's all wet.

Boy

Boy
wild, boisterous
fighting, winning, whining
slingshots, swords / hugs, kisses
smiling, enjoying, needing
mild, mannered
Man

On William Shakespeare's Whole Portfolio

Finally, brothers . . . if anything is excellent or praiseworthy—
fix your mind on *these* things. (Philippians 4:8.NIV *Emphasis mine.*)

I boycott all his multi-acted song.
Admittedly, his writing's graced with skill,
but even when the trees at hand are strong
you can't conclude the forest isn't ill.
I shan't pretend that reading his *Macbeth*
has left me feeling well and satisfied,
nor that *Othello*'s spectre of cold death
left me without warm thoughts of suicide.
The world's replete with tales rife with deceit
and every devilish atrocity;
so, why deplete my mind by yarns complete
with crime, like Willy's word monstrosity,
when I can concentrate on everything
the lovely, lordly, bright and blessed will bring?

On a Child's Death

At their child's deathbed,
they, not so very long ago
separated
by harsh words, hurt feelings
and legal documents,
finally found the strength
to comfort each other,
to cry together—to share,
behind laughing sobs,
fond memories of cherished moments
together.
Could their child have been the one
to hold those words and feelings at bay?

On Divorce

What is divorce?
Is it circumcision:
the ceremonial removal
of unwanted flesh?
Perhaps it's amputation:
removing a dead limb,
or maybe it's emasculation:
dismantling the central part
to tame a mutt—

but does that really keep him from straying?

Last Requests

We sure been havin' lots of visitors
of late. I ain't necessarily
complainin', don't y'know. I'm glad to have
so many friends, but let me ask you, please,
jus' how the hell they s'pose't' help me heal?
No, don't you "Now, Dear" me. I ain't in the mood.
I can't get out of bed to say "Hello,"
and it's humiliatin' having them
in here to see me all cooped up in bed;
it makes me feel weak, and I ain't weak.
It only takes a little bit of patience
to wait to visit an old man while he's
recuperatin' in the privacy
of his own home, his missus at his side—
some patience and a bit o' common sense.
And some o' them folks I ain't chanced to see
since we was kids out on my parents' farm.
Now, I like reminiscin' just as much
as anybody else, but, criminitly!
I gotta save m' strength so's I can heal.
I got m' work that's needin' to be done:
them broken wheels ain't gunna fix themselves;
I promised Chuck I'd help him mend his roof;
and you and I were gunna dig a garden
around your Mama's apple tree this year
so's we can plant some flowers in the spring.
We'll have to do it soon 'cause winter's just
around the bend, and it'll take us both.

Why can't they visit when I'm strong again?
Jus' tell'm, "Thanks for stoppin' by. He'll see
you when he's feelin' better. Come again."
I simply need to rest in peace an' quiet.
Now, jus' a minute, I ain't mad at you.
There ain't no cause for cryin'; I ain't mad.
It's just that I'm perplexed by all of this.
Here, come on over. Let me hug ya. There;
you always feel better with a hug.
You know what I would love? I'd love a bit
of that delicious soup you made last night.
Would you be bothered heatin' up a bowl?
Why, thank you, Darlin'. I'll just rest my eyes
so's I can sit up when it's time to eat. . . .
With all these visitors and cryin', hmph!
you'd think a fella' can't get well again.

The Flim-Flam Man

The flim-flam man can
hold up people with a scam,
make the wishy-washy man
falter from his well-laid plan.

His hodge-podge of mumbo-jumbo—
a quickly-speaking sing-song combo—
mesmerizes moppet Dumbo,
holding him like one in limbo.

This cracker-jack lives to distract;
razzle-dazzle's half his act.
One hand to show, one to extract
cash or cards—whatever's packed.

His jingle-jangle's flashy really,
making victims feel silly.
It's tip-top art; there's nothing frilly—
stealing livings willy-nilly.

Po ë Tree

The phrase, "Geometry,"
is quoted by an adultery
or often by a symmetry
and even by a ministry,
an ancestry, an artistry,
a sentry, a pleasantry,
a peasantry, a poetry—
an entire forestry!
but never by an infantry
(not to be a bigotry);
an infantry is notary at all;
it's a seed.

Book of Poems

I bought a second-hand
book of poetry—
well read
with a bunch dog-eared pages.
"Man, that ticks me off!
What fool . . . ?"
I said scowling, and I uncreased each corner.
But when I'd finished reading the entire book,
I found that I had marked again
the very same pages.

Late Night Among Friends

Late at night, in the quiet of the home
we clustered close like kernels on a cob
and laughed and giggled at our stories and
the stupid questions preteens find
so serious when parents aren't around.
Huddled in the attic where Freddie and Lizzie
lived more vividly in dust and mold,
we shared as we dared, with flash-lighted faces,
gross gossip and goblin tales, testing
to top the other tellers. We took pride
that we had only once been told—up through
the heating vents—to "please keep it down;"
another bodiless voice to bolster our game.

"D'y'think they're doin' it?" One asked,
choking on a chuckle.

"If they were doin' it tonight,
they'd *want* us loud," another said
and brought us all to laughter.

"I don't think they do it anymore, do you?
I mean, they're in their forties, for cryin' out loud!"

"So what?
Jaimy Hanson's baby brother was born
when his dad was *fifty*, so *they* still do it—
at least, they did eleven months ago."

"My parents were in their forties when I was born,
and they still do it; I heard'm."

"Oh, gross, man!"
                    "Yuck!"
                              "Wha'd'ya do?"

"Turned up the tunes and read a book; what else?"

"Wow! Your parents were forty when you were born?"

"What of it?"
                    "It seems so weird."
                                        "Yeah, our parents
were in their twenties."

                    "My mom was twenty-eight.
Don't know how old my dad was."

                                   "Mine was thirty."

"My mom was dead when I was born," I said.

     The laughter stopped—the breathing stopped,
and every disbelieving stare fell like stone on me,
so I stammered, unsure of what to say.

     "Get real!"
     "Yeah!"
     "How could you be here
if your mom died before you were even born?"

     "Come on!"
     "Answer that!"

"On the night that I was born, my mother's
boyfriend beat her bloody and left her lyin'
there to die. When someone got her help,
her time was up already. Doctors didn't do a thing
but take me out and cover up her face.
She wasn't much older than us.
Well, that's the way I'm told. Jake and Mary—
they just raise me."

We all sat silent for a spell.
No one even looked at me.

I had over-stepped some unspoken bounds:
too close, perhaps, or too gross.
Thank God another finally found a voice:

"So, y'think Jake and Mary still do it?"

After a chortle, we all laughed again.

The New Pleasure
(after Kahlil Gibran)

When I had finished making my
        unprecedented pleasure,
an angel and a demon came
        demanding search and seizure.

But since it could not go both ways,
        and they were under pressure,
they made my brain their battle line—
        each ear their embrasure.

They sat at ease to fight it out;
        each promised full disclosure
of his insights and arguments
        across a cerebral fissure.

So both as one on either side
        with effort, at their leisure,
discussed its worth with calm assent—
        its faults in heated censure.

And when they had completed their
        debating in full measure,
the one conceded, "It's a sin."
        the other, "It's a treasure."

Response to "Plato Told"[11]

True

General Sherman[12]
told him
as did Christ
and Plato
before him

but

he needs the bite of
lead
the bodies of the
dead
destruction of his
head

Nothing's taught
in what is
said

Nothing learned
if only
read

Parachute Play Time

Back in my younger days of school, my class
enjoyed the rare occasions Teacher brought
his coloured parachute for play. *En masse*
we clutched the circled edge, pulled it taut,
and with it caught the playground ball that, when
we raised or dropped our arms, would roll about
the ruffling rim. And in our favourite spin
we'd send it straight across with laughs and shouts.
Today, the frosty mountains where I live—
they seem to me the grasping knuckles of
those laughing children lifted high to give
the parachute of sky the thrust to shove
that shining playground ball from end to end;
together hands and chute and sphere ascend.

Outlanders

The world that they called home is burning cold:
A moon in orbit 'round a larger moon
in orbit 'round a planet, all controlled
by suns as faint as distant stars, at noon.
And yet, these folks had no great needs to meet:
They framed grand homes with girders forged of strips
of ice, shaped and sealed by candle heat.
And of that same design they molded ships
to venture through the dark of outer space
and greet the torrid life on other orbs.
They found one with a friendly, blue-hued face,
and boldly settled on the surface that absorbs
those frozen hulls—a vat of fervent potion;
they burned to death near Terra's Arctic ocean.

Silent Night in the Grass

Up into the stars—
tiny bits of twinkling time
eyeing, gleaning hours.

O Christmas Tree

"They're already dead,"
I console my little girl.
"What about next year's?"
she asks me. "They're not dead yet."
So we're off to buy a fake.

Limerick

A limerick's not fit for the books
of writers concerned with their looks.
 Most poets who write'm
 emphatically hide'm
or secretly share them like crooks.

A sonnet is a fourteen-line, rhymed poem in iambic pentameter. "Pentameter" means that there are–ideally–ten syllables per line, and each line has five stressed syllables. "Iambic" indicates that, in the construction of each line (NOT in the presentation of each line), every even-numbered syllable is stressed. There are, roughly, four types of sonnets, each identified by its rhyme scheme, but any fourteen-line rhymed poem in iambic pentameter is a sonnet.

I feel very blessed to have been the creator of my own rhyme scheme. I don't use it exclusively, as Spenser did with his own rhyme scheme, but it is mine, and I always feel myself sit up a little straighter when I think of myself as having created my own rhyme scheme for the sonnet: AABA BBCB CCDC DD.

It is an unfortunate fact that a sonneteer is regarded as something of a hack in contemporary literary circles, as an artist who paints on 8 ½ x 11 inch paper might be. I'm not the only sonneteer in this generation, but all of us are "in a class of our own," and, in this case, that's not considered a good thing. Ah, me.

I've always been something of an old-fashioned boy. As a result, sonnets appeal to me; they always have. And it's my contention that one day the sonnet will reclaim its place in popularity; it did in 1803 thanks to Wordsworth and Coleridge, and that comeback lasted until the1960's, ending, essentially, with the deaths of Robert Frost and E. E. Cummings. The sonnet's history and my praise of the poetic form are both summed up in the following three sonnets, each of which uses my own rhyme scheme. In fact, the second of these is the first one I wrote with my rhyme scheme. In the third one, I made a variation of my own rhyme scheme.

On the Sonnet I

From Dryden until Wordsworth Sonnet fell
from favour, so hiding well, she went to dwell
in springs and pools where, bobbing up her eye
and nose, she'd scan the line for sight or smell
of careless men, who, now and then, would lie
beneath a tree and, sighing, ask the sky,
"What does she see in *him*?" Then Sonnet struck!
and carried off her prey with one last cry.
From Wordsworth up through Cummings Sonnet's luck
held sway; again though, rarely can she pluck
an unsuspecting schmuck or seldom snack
on poets who just want to earn a buck.
Yet Sonnet, soon, shall rise to the attack,
fill in the crack, replace what writers lack.

On the Sonnet II

I'm well aware of what Ben Jonson said:
Employing rhyme in poetry is dead
for Greek and Roman writers used it not,
and rhyming wrenches reason from the head.
John Milton said the same thing when he taught
that paradise is lost when rhyme is got—
denouncing rhyme as just a frilly bonnet
veiling vulgar verse of little thought.
But had the Greeks and Romans known the sonnet,
they'd have gladly hunted rhyme to crown it—
living trophies captured and refined
to master artistry and so to spawn it.
Free verse has its place, I am resigned,
but poets can't break free if not confined.

On the Sonnet III

"Iambic pentameter?!"—a bellowed mew—
"It's lifeless! Bid that dead technique adieu!"
Thus blustered critic, Ezra Pound—a cry
from sentiments that simply are untrue.
And, "it's where old professors go to die."
This statement, quipped by poet, Robert Bly,
expresses pangs not altogether new
but is, in humble honesty, a lie.
Ms. Sonnet, our poetic schoolmarm, earned
respect when, with her stern approach, we learned
to deepen thought by capping writing space.
Go visit her and see that she has churned
great poetry from you, and then replace
your attitude with gratitude and grace.

When I Met You . . .
(A Love Poem)

. . . Admiration and Appreciation
married in my heart and bred.
They named their baby girl Attraction,
and as she grew, became Affection.
When she was old enough to wed,
her married name was Adoration.

Harsh Words

When harsh words leave your mouth,
they saunter down the street
in their Gothic garb, smoking.
You can't command them back. They're gone.
They meet up with their buddies,
huddle together
and laugh at you.
Then they turn their backs on you
and run off to do their damage.
You have no authority, no control. They're gone.
You should have exercised your strength
before they grew too strong for you to hold.

The Commoner

I squander my earnings—
    don't give a damn—
and bury my memory in whiskey;
It keeps me forgetting
    the thing that I am
and the man that I never will be.

Unhappy Limerick

He had a few drinks in the car
and died on his way from the bar.
He drank by himself
with his life on a shelf
and peace of mind frightfully far.

A Beggar Muses on His Good Fortune
If a man will not work, he shall not eat. (2 Thessalonians 3:10)

I earned a living, once upon a time,
but now I roam the evening streets while folks
maneuver past my eyes, for if we meet,
they know that they're obliged to reach inside
their pockets to retrieve those little coins
they'd hoped to plug the parking meter with,
or save to buy the kids a gum ball since
they were so good while Mom and Dad were out.
I make them feel guilty down inside;
they know they're better off than I am, so
they have responsibilities—to me.
But they don't know that I, of all the beggars
downtown tonight, am better off than any;
I'm nowhere near as needy as the rest,
and that's why I must work so hard to beg
my way through life: to keep the real beggars
away from those who give so easily.
See, I could work, if I were so inclined;
I have a university degree,
and I could make good money—I have before—
I could, say, find a job, pay my bills,
buy a house or rent, feed myself
and even feed my family—if I wanted,
but then I'm forced to ask myself, "Why?"
My income stood a stout six figures strong,
and I was kind with it; I'm not a Scrooge.

So when a family came to me to beg
for finances to save their dying child,
did I hold back? Not on your life! I gave
them every cent they needed, even more!
But when my weakness got found out, they all
came hoarding by for money, "Help me pay
them off!" "Give me money for tuition!"
"I have a dying grandma!" I gave and gave,
and they kept coming, like bad songs played time
and time again on some new radio station
that hasn't any decent tunes to play.
So then, one day, I kissed my wife and kids
goodbye and walked away from everything.
I still have on the same old clothes; they're little
more than rags by now, but I don't mind.
The only thing I worry for is food,
and these good folks have paid for every meal.
By simply holding up an empty palm,
I reach inside a man more deeply than
the hand of God; I grab the heart and squeeze
out all that stingy generosity.
And they're the ones who used to beg from me.
I used to bless them with my money; now
I bless them with an altruistic heart:
"God love you, sir." "You're Grace incarnate, sir."
I help myself and help them see themselves
as people kind and caring. It's not as though
I'm stealing, God forbid! Consider this:
I only take what's mine; if this is stealing,
who better could I steal from than beggars—
from those who need it so much more than I,
and, really, who would give a cent for them?

The French composer, Camille Saint-Saëns (1835-1921) wrote one of his better-known musical masterpieces, *Danse Macabre*, from the inspiration of the poem of the same title, written by French poet, Henri Cazalis (1840-1909). Since I am a musician as well as a poet, I have set myself the task of either translating or re-creating as many of these music-inspiring poems as I can. "Danse Macabre" is my first, translated from the French.

Danse Macabre

T'click, t'click, t'click. Death taps a tomb—
His fleshless foot begins a boney beat,
and at the height this chilly night of gloom
a spritely dance he fiddles—grim and meet.

He scrapes the strings and scratches out a lead;
The dead arise at the chilling cries he plays.
Those bones, those bones, those dry bones, they all heed
their lord and dance as in less dismal days.

T'click, t'click, t'clack. They skip and prance.
But two hold back—both hoping to refresh
their naked bones in a horizontal dance
and seek anew the pleasures of the flesh.

They say that she was born a noble lass,
that he descended from a line more base.
Their rotting rags, though, give no hint of class;
their skinless bones betray no sign of race.

T'click, t'click, t'clack. And with a hop
Death turns aside to hide a knowing grin.
He scratches out a tune and doesn't stop
the howling yowling of his violin.

T'click, t'click, t'click. Yes, hand in hand
the others lark, freed from the sombre grave.
In Death alone is no one's passion banned.
Why, Royalty can even romp with Slave.

But hush! Each drops his partner's boney hand
to break and scatter! Ah, the rooster sings!
A lovely night for those in every land.
Live on, Death! For equality he brings.

The Photo

. . . Now, that's a picture of my baby girl
you're holding. She was, maybe, five?—or was
she six then?—practicing her moves for her
ballet recital—or . . . could be gymnastics.
It was so long ago; the outfits were
the same—pink leotards and naked feet . . .
I still remember wrestling with that shot:
I used my brand-new Cannon A-L I;
It's antiquated now, but in its day
it held its own among the very best.
The light was bad because of all the kids
positioned in a circle all around her;
there, in the background; can you see them there?
I had to use a special flash to dodge
that "red-eye" glow. These days, with our computers,
those kinds of things can be removed, but then . . .
You had to be a good photographer.
You understand, of course, I'm using terms
a layman, like yourself, would likely use.
And just check out that pose! I'd watched her routine
so many times, just to get her in
a shot like this! It's like a poem, somehow.
And then there were the contrasts in the colours,
the squaring of the image to consider,
and finding just the perfect spot to angle
this flawless shot . . . I had it all arranged.
I'm really proud of how well it turned out.

Antonio Vivaldi (1678-1741) is best known today for his famous suite of four concerto grossi: *The Four Seasons.* The "Concerto grosso" (the plural is "concerto grossi"), Latin for "large concert," is a musical form that was popular during the Baroque era (c. 1600-1750). It is an orchestral piece of three movements (three "chapters," if you will) with a number of solos or duets during the whole. Usually, the solos are for the violin, but they can also be for the cello or viola. This form was ultimately replaced in the Classical era (c. 1750-1800) by the concerto, which is a solo for one instrument with orchestral accompaniment.

But Vivaldi didn't just write the music. In order for his listeners to be better able to interpret his music—to understand why a certain melody reflected a certain season in Vivaldi's ears—he also wrote four sonnets, one for each season, to accompany his music. Since each of Vivaldi's *Four Seasons* concerto grossi has three movements, each sonnet is sub-divided.

In my translations that follow, I've indicated each sub-division with an asterisk (*) before each separate part other than the opening, so the first asterisk indicates the beginning of the text for the second movement, and the second asterisk indicates the text for the third movement, which will always conclude at the end of line twelve. (I have reserved the final couplet to use as a transition to the following sonnet.)

You will notice that each sonnet is not necessarily evenly divided for the movements of each concerto grosso. This is Vivaldi's doing, not mine.

I. Spring

As Spring ascends her predecessor's throne
and Cold succumbs to passion by and by,
the little streams warm up their merry tone
and, with the birds, sing praises to the Sky.
For even when she's cloaked in sable clouds,
and Lightning thunders, heralding a storm,
the Sky will shortly shed her homely shrouds
and, standing in her nakedness, keep warm.
*The shepherds doze contentedly, their chore
entrusted to their faithful canine friends,
*while townsfolk sing the tale—with a bagpipe score—
of Spring's return and the joy her presence lends.
But all the merriment of Spring shall slow
when Summer's brazened bugle begins to blow.

II. Summer

When Summer's brazened bugle begins to blow
on all who live beneath that blazing ball,
the cuckoo, finch and dove decry their woe,
together raising up a tiny squall.
And in her harshness, Summer takes their tweet
and multiplies it, first to breeze and then to gale;
then all can mourn the loss of Summer's heat
as gentle rain transforms to hellish hail.
*The shepherd naps no more, for buzzing flies
keep darting near his ear as if they know.
*And whether dreading clear or cloudy skies
the farmers pray their crops proceed to grow.
The time is short, though, to endure these pains
as Summer ends, and Autumn takes the reins.

III. Autumn

As Summer ends and Autumn takes the reins
the farmers celebrate with song and dance
that all their stores are stocked with all their grains,
then gather to their wives for sweet romance.
*Contentedly they leave their toils behind
and revel in the season's honey air
for several days—perhaps a week—inclined
to settle back and live without a care.
*And then at dawn one day, they sally forth
with bows and howling dogs to stalk their prey.
The watchful quarry flees for all he's worth,
'til Death conducts him safely from the fray.
Then all men hide—their families safe at hand—
while Winter wends his way throughout the land.

IV. Winter

While Winter wends his way throughout the land
we find ourselves so burned by caustic cold
in his outdoor demesne (best left unmanned),
our trembling can by no means be controlled.
*Indoors, alone, are people's bodies warmed
by family, food and fire while winds without
demand our fuelling flesh. That's why they've swarmed:
to claim our lives since man is not so stout.
*So no one dares to walk a winter path
without a friend to save him if he falls,
lest he should quickly learn of Winter's wrath
and prematurely wander Heaven's Halls.
But even Winter reaps what he has sown
as Spring ascends her predecessor's throne.

The Death of the Ace

It may have been "the war to end all wars,"
just not the way we thought it would at first.
The dawn of war, with Cain and Abel, proved
that warfare is a face-to-face ordeal,
and combat didn't change for centuries.
The weapons and defences may have changed
as time progressed or as our cultures moved,
but always is it true that each man knows
his foe; he sees the face of his opponent—
the pain, the shock, the utter sense of loss
in each man's eye as he is taken out,
and each surviving soldier has to face
those faces every night in every dream
from that point on, in sickness and in health,
for richer and for poorer, for bad to worse,
so long as he alone proceeds to live.
       The bow and arrow didn't change a thing;
a target must be close enough to see.
The rifle shoots a greater distance, but
the soldier's eye still must take its aim.
And that's how people always fought their wars,
and so we did when people took to the air.
How many times did I salute the man
whom I would very soon condemn to death?
How often did my foe return in kind?
Like football teams who greet before the game.
We knew each other—even enemies—
if not by name, then by his reputation:
how many victories, how many planes
he had survived before our pending duel.
We each respected each, regardless of
his home, and every time one died, I mourned.

I stood among the best of all of them,
the Aces in that war, with victories to spare;
we didn't even have an air force yet.
Oh, I remember every one of them—
no, not the victories—the men I killed,
and it's been almost eighty years ago.
    To know your enemy before he falls—
that's what makes war a thing to be avoided;
that's what makes it ugly, painful, vile.
not like the cozy anonymity
we cloak ourselves with in these 'modern' times
since we've 'evolved' and 'civilized ourselves.'
No longer do our pilots slaughter men
in dog fights; there's no man for them to see;
they shoot the aircraft while they're miles apart.
And even when they're close enough to see
each other, there's no face to see; they hide
themselves in helmets, goggles, masks or speed.
And war, my friends, is no more dangerous
or frightening or ugly than a game;
we're children playing 'cops and robbers,' safe
behind our fences in our own back yards.
    I'm ninety-six this year,[13] and I will try
no more to change your minds or how you live.
I'm old and ill, and I am checking out,
like all the other Aces, from the world.
I wish you luck and hope that some of you
will live to see your ninety-sixth year pass.

A Single Day to Wallow in Self Pity

Today my heart goes out to me alone,
and I shall take this single day to groan
beneath the beastly burdens that I bear.
It may appear my heart has turned to stone,
but I'm turned inward, nursing traumas there.
If you have aches, I simply cannot care
today—but just today. Leave me to hurt
and wallow in self pity and despair
this once; forgive me if my words are curt;
don't hold me in contempt if I should blurt
out grievings or obnoxiously complain.
(I've held my tongue while you were flinging dirt.)
Tomorrow I will be myself again
and bare with you the world's grief and pain.

Poem

This is what I saw:
a young Asian woman,
alone, sad,
marching barefoot up a road
through a forest.
It might have been a pleasant walk—
an affable breeze ambled through the trees,
the sun sprinkled starlets on the ground,
the air breathed fresh, content, alive—
it might have been a pleasant walk,
but her babies had been taken from her—
she didn't know why,
she didn't know where—
by a force far more tremendous
than her own
motherly might,
and now that force
made her march,
she didn't know where,
she didn't know why.
She had wondered
if she might ever see her babies again;
now she knew.
There were others marching by force
sparsely populating the road,
paved with sticks and leaves
in various stages of decay.
A vast variety of fungi
spread unabashedly across the moist soil—
as blithely oblivious as Nature ever was—
as they marched
separately, silently, obediently,
their eyes cast down,
their thoughts turned inward.

In time,
she was joined by a friend;
who had also just been made
childless.
They knew each other
they cared for each other,
and for a time,
they silently comforted each other,
and their grief abated—
for a time.
Finally, she thrust her palms
to her ears,
pressing as though squeezing
the tears from her eyes.
Her friend understood—
without a single word
she understood:
"I can hear my babies cry."
Her friend heard without a word,
and spoke just as voicelessly:
"Yes, I hear my babies, too.
We will walk
together,
and give each other strength."

They held each other's hands.
All four hands clasped before them
as they walked and wept
when three shots rang out
and she screamed out in horrific,
agonizing, heart-wrenching pain,
hobbled off the road and dropped—
confused, frightened—in ceaseless,
incomparable pain.
    Her friend walked on in terror,
in solitude,
and the man with the rifle
strode past;
he had gained no pleasure,
he had gained no satisfaction.
In his heart was just his uniform.
He had given no warning;
he had given no cause;
he had given no command.
    She could not die.
The others rushed past her,
filled with compassion,
wanting to help,
unable to help,
afraid to help.
She wretched, she writhed
in agonizing cries.
"Oh please! Someone shoot her.
Someone kill her.
Stop that abominable screaming."
No one spoke,
but shared the thought
from one to the next
like a bottle of whiskey.

Finally,
after minute upon minute of
God-awful screaming,
three more joyless, thoughtless
uniformed rifles offered
seven additional rounds.
She sank to the ground
looking up at nothing,
vacantly smearing blood from her eyes.
Then she—and her babies—fell silent.
    This is what I saw.
If it can be dreamed,
it has probably happened.
If it has happened,
it can happen again.
God help us.
God help us.

This is the first poem that I ever translated. I was studying French at college in North Dakota, and my instructor brought this poem by Jaques Prévert (1900-1977) into the class to test us, just to see if we could understand it. I have to say that I was sent to the head of the class for the day when I wrote this translation.

The Message

The door that someone opened
The door that someone closed
The chair where someone sat
The cat that someone caressed

The fruit that someone bit
The letter that someone read
The chair someone throws
The door someone opens

The path someone runs
The forest someone crosses
The river someone breathes
The hospital where that someone lies dead.

The End of Captain Hook

The Captain shook his upturned hook because
his rival, Peter Pan, had won: "What does
a boy command that Captain Hook cannot?
My crew adore him even! How it gnaws
at me to think that dirty, little snot
would leave me nothing but this ancient yacht;
a bursting brig; a single, trusted mate—
I'll waste no rounds to have the others shot."
He called this order to his crewman: "Klate!
Throw each disloyal, witless sailor as bait
to that ubiquitous croc." "Every sailor?"
inquired Klate. "Yes, Smee too," the hate
in Hook commanded him. "Well, as you say, sir,"
said Klate and shoved his captain to the water.

A Love Poem

EDITH: Did you do something wrong? Are you afraid of something? Whatever it is, let me help.

KIRK: "Let me help . . ." A hundred years, or so, from now, I believe, a famous [writer] will write a classic using that theme. He'll recommend those three words even over, "I love you."

From "The City on the Edge of Forever." Dir. Joseph Pevney. *Star Trek*. April 6, 1969.

You say, "I love you." I believe it's true,
but not because you say it like you do:
so often and so heartfelt. No, but I
believe it for another thought that you
repeat to me each time you hear me sigh,
or when I cry, and every time I try
to deal with issues on my own: you say,
"Let me help," and I know I can't deny
you love me; you commit yourself to stay
with me, take action for me and display
your love. So let this little phrase entwine
us always to declare Dependence Day:
"Let me help." "Let me help." Our hearts combine
in acts of love and prove our love divine.

What's In a Name?

I come from an average family:
a mom, a dad, three kids, a dog.
I have an older brother, a younger sister,
both born mid-century, like me.

My modest home-town lies smack-dab
in the heart of the mid-west;
I graduated from high-school there
with my GPA dead on the median.

My eyes are blue, my blood type "O,"
my hair a curly, dish-water blond.
My I.Q. is moderate; my build
is common, my achievements—indistinct.

Never an extremist—always centered—
(not a Ptolemaic[14] "centred," obscure:
never first, never last: hidden, unseen)

I'm a right-handed, good old-fashioned,
White Anglo-Saxon Protestant,
red-blooded, American, "Yes, Ma'am" boy.

Every obvious feature embodies
modality, typifies "blah;"
even "Mittendorf" means "mid-town."

Endnotes

1   'The Rape of Lucretia:' A tale in Roman literature that tells of a prince who is so captivated by Lucretia—his friend's wife and a princess herself—that he goes to her at night and confesses his undying love for her, begs for her love, then, when she denies him, he rapes her violently.

2   Frieze: a horizontal band comprised of several low-relief sculptures telling a story. They are often found around the cornices of Greek temples.

3   Pharaoh: an Egyptian king. It was widely believed that they became gods after their deaths.

4   "this land is mine. God gave / this land to me" quotes the opening line of the song, "Exodus," (Lyrics: Pat Boone, Musical score: Ernest Gold) from the film of the same name. The song's persona, however, is Jewish.

5   According to the original Greek myths, Themis, the goddess of law, prophesied that the son of Thetis (a nereid or water goddess) would be greater than his father, whomever that father might be; the prophesy was ultimately fulfilled in Achilles, who was a far greater warrior than his father, Peleus, had been, and Peleus was, himself, no slouch. Zeus, who was never known for his fidelity, had had eyes for Thetis, but this prophesy dissuaded him from her lest he should one day be forced to abdicate his throne. In composing this sonnet, I wanted to demonstrate what it might look like–what it might really mean–for Zeus's son to be greater than his father.

[6]   Zeus was the son of Kronos (A. K. A Saturn), and Kronos was the son of Uranus. Uranus was seen as evil by Kronos because he (Uranus) confined some of his own deformed sons to Tartarus, which is said to be the gloomiest part of the underworld, as far under Earth as Earth is under the sky. To avenge his siblings, Kronos castrated his father and confined him to Tartarus. In turn, Kronos, seeing all of his offspring as potential threats to his kingship, ate them (Poseidon, Hades and Hera) in tandem as they were born. Only Zeus was saved, and when he was old enough, he rescued his siblings from his father's belly and confined Kronos to Tartarus.

[7]   Sic semper proditores: Latin, "Thus always to traitors."

[8]   SPAD: French, single-seat fighter biplane used during World War I, designed by Louis Béchereau of the Société Pour L'Aviation et ses Dérivés (Society for Aviation and its Derivatives).

[9]   Eugene Jacques Bullard (1894-1961): American born WWI Flying Ace who flew with French allegiance. He was awarded the *Croix de Guerre* (The Cross of War) and the *Légion d'honneur* (Legion of Honour), and was the independent victor in at least five aerial battles (dog fights) after having been barred from flying for the U. S. because of racism. He is now, however, proudly counted among American flying aces.

[10]   Phillis Wheatley (c. 1753-1784) was born in Africa, but was abducted and sold into slavery. She was bought by the Wheately family of Boston, Massachusetts, who taught her to read and write. In spite of her status as a slave and as a woman, she became the first published Black poet in America and toured England with her poetry and won the praise of King George III and General George Washington among other high-ranking dignitaries.

[11]   See "Plato told," a poem by E. E. Cummings.

[12]   It was General William Tecumseh Sherman (1820-1891) who was apparently quoted as saying, "War is hell."

[13]   Arthur Raymond Brooks (1895-1991) was the last surviving WWI flying ace in North America.

[14] Ptolemaic: having to do with Ptolemy (Claudius Ptolemaeus c. AD 90- c. AD168), who, in the height of the Roman Empire, postulated that the earth was located in the centre of the universe, suggesting that the sun, moon, planets and stars revolved around the earth, and thus, Earth is not only the centre of the universe but also, subsequently, the centre of attention of all the gods and goddesses. In my poem, I want to suggest that, while "centred" can mean either to stand out as an apex—a peak; (this would be the "Ptolemaic 'centred'"), the same word can also mean "befogged" or "blended in," (the meaning I'm referring to).

Incidentally, Ptolemy's erroneous model of the universe was adapted into the Christian faith during the medieval era and remained the cornerstone of Christian doctrine and dogma until well after Nicolaus Copernicus (1473-1543) proved, in (circa) 1508, that the sun was the centre of our solar system (or the universe, to the medieval mind), and even after his findings were confirmed by Galileo Galilee (1564-1642) a century later, in 1610.